Contents

Weekly Units

sh

Action
Place your index finger against your lips, and say *sh.*

am
get
clap
shop
fish
shut
wish
I
the
shampoo

Write an <sh> word in each fish and draw a picture to match.

Dictation

1......................................

2......................................

3......................................

4......................................

5......................................

6......................................

7...

8...

9...

Rainbow capital letters

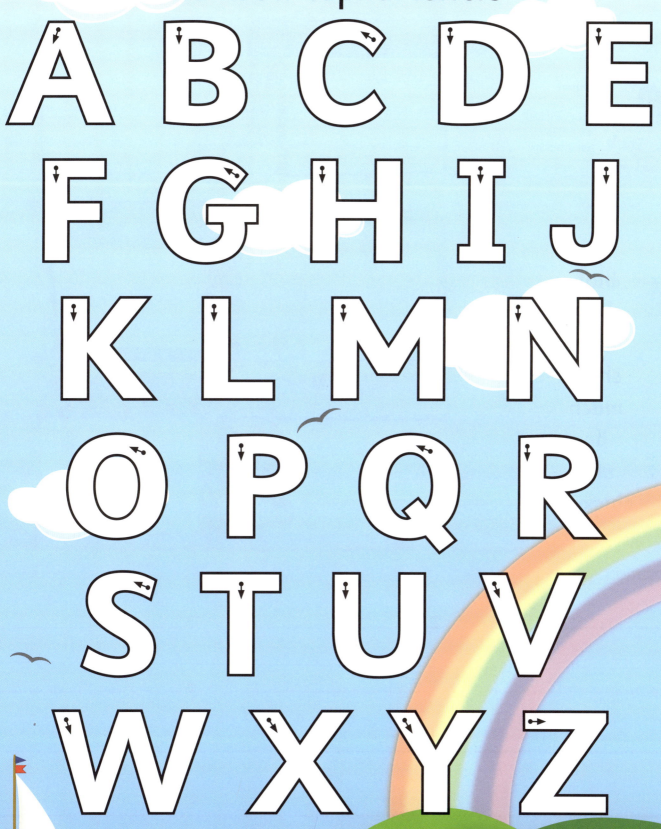

ch

 Action
Move your arms as if you are a steam train, and say *ch*.

if
hot
blot
chips
lunch
chest
much
he
she
chicken

Write a <ch> word in each chest and draw a picture to match.

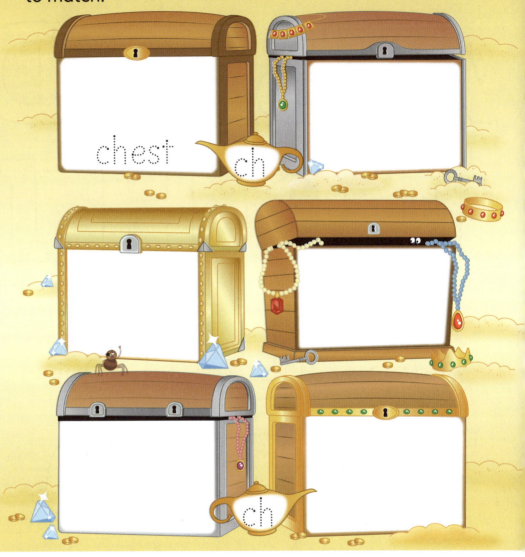

Dictation

1...................................

2...................................

3...................................

4...................................

5...................................

6...................................

7...

8...

9...

4

Sentences

Put the words in the right order to make a sentence about the picture.

A _____

Put the words in the right order and color the picture.

th

Action
Stick out your tongue, a little for *th* and further for *th*.

us
sad
flag
this
with
that
thank
me
we
thinking

Write a ‹th› word in each thought bubble and draw a picture to match.

Dictation

1.....................................

2.....................................

3.....................................

4.....................................

5.....................................

6.....................................

7...

8...

9...

Are these sentences correct? Write out each sentence correctly on the line.

1. the dog is spotty.

_____

2. The duck swims on the.

_____

3. I sleep in a bunk bed.

_____

4. i like. fried eggs

_____

5. They are playing.

_____

ng

Action
Pretend to lift a heavy weight above your head, and say *ng*.

in
leg
glad
ring
sang
strong
lung
be
was
length

Write an <ng> word in each ring and draw a picture to match.

Dictation

1...

2...

3...

4...

5...

6...

7...

8...

9...

8

Capital letters

Write the capital letter next to each lower-case letter.

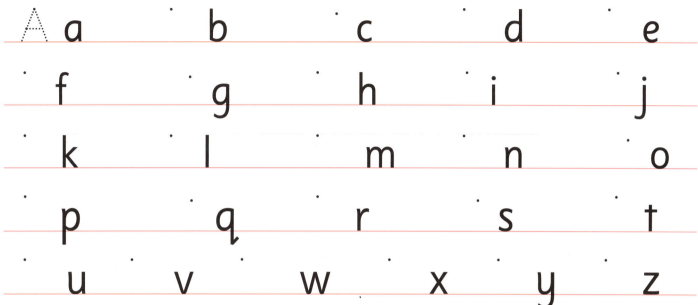

A a   b   c   d   e

f   g   h   i   j

k   l   m   n   o

p   q   r   s   t

u   v   w   x   y   z

Join each capital letter to the matching lower-case letter.

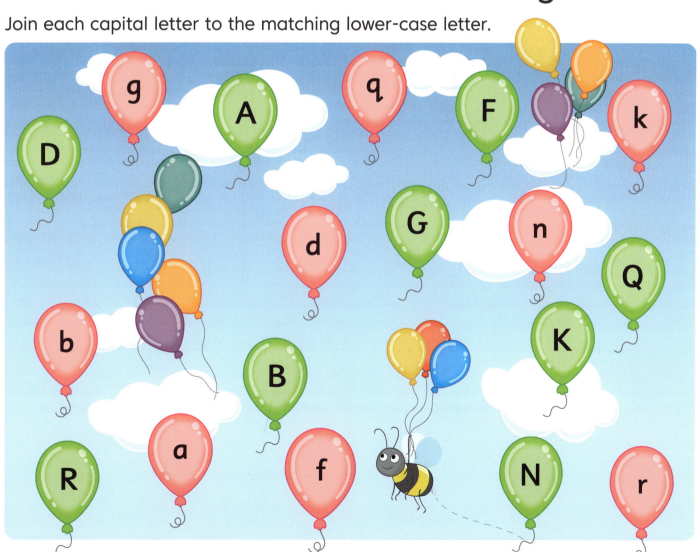

9

qu

Action
Make a duck's beak with your hands, and say *qu*.

on
but
plum
quick
quiz
queen
squid
to
do
squirrel

Write a <qu> word in each duck and draw a picture to match.

Dictation

1..

2..

3..

4..

5..

6..

7..

8..

9..

10

Proper nouns

Action
Touch your forehead with your index and middle fingers.

Draw pictures of you and your teacher and write your names underneath.

me

my teacher

_____

_____

_____

_____

Write your school's address on the envelope.

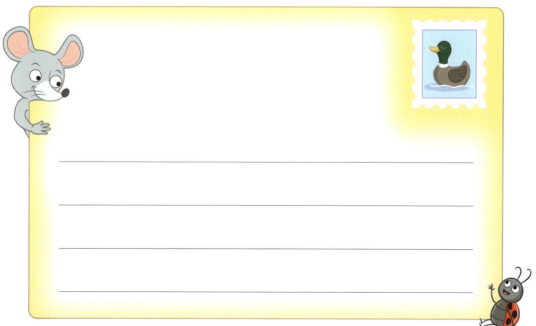

ar

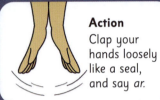

Action
Clap your hands loosely like a seal, and say *ar*.

at
yes
slug
arm
hard
scarf
card
are
all
farmyard

Write an <ar> word in each star and draw a picture to match.

Dictation

1...................................

2...................................

3...................................

4...................................

5...................................

6...................................

7..

8..

9..

12

Common nouns

Action
Put your hand on your forehead.

Draw three pictures and write the nouns underneath.

_____   _____   _____

Write a noun in the gap to finish each sentence and draw its picture in the box.

1. The _____ is black.

2. I throw the _____.

3. A _____ can swim.

4. I like to eat _____.

Short vowels

vowel hand

dog
bran
Monday
Tuesday
Wednesday
Thursday
Friday
you
your
Saturday

Fill each container with short vowel words. Write /a/ words in the bag, /e/ words in the net, /i/ words in the bin, /o/ words in the box, and /u/ words in the mug.

Dictation

1......................................

2......................................

3......................................

4......................................

5......................................

6......................................

7...

8...

9...

Alphabetical order

Write the capital letter next to each lower-case letter.

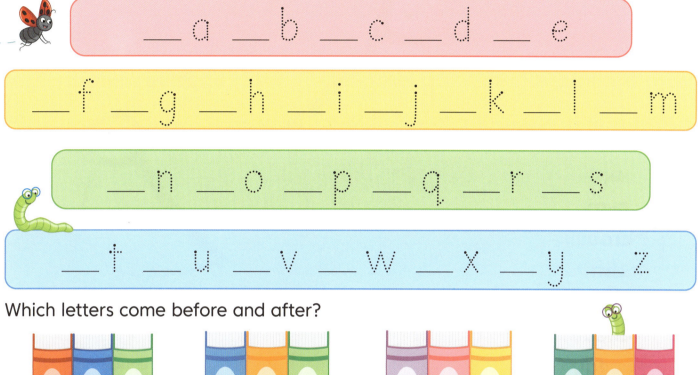

__ a __ b __ c __ d __ e

__ f __ g __ h __ i __ j __ k __ l __ m

__ n __ o __ p __ q __ r __ s

__ t __ u __ v __ w __ x __ y __ z

Which letters come before and after?

R S T

K

Y

C

V

F

M

B

Put these sets of letters into alphabetical order.

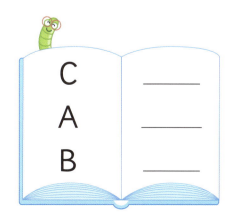

C
A
B

___
___
___

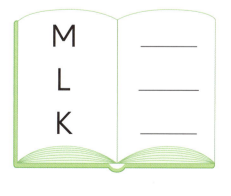

M
L
K

___
___
___

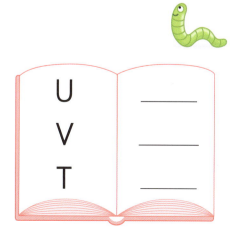

U
V
T

___
___
___

15

Double letters

ss ff
ll zz

up
man
crab
cliff
puffin
buzz
shell
come
some
crossroads

Write a double letter word in each shape and draw a picture to match.

Dictation

1..

2..

3..

4..

5..

6..

7...

8...

9...

16

a or an?

Say the word for each picture. Write **an** if the word begins with a vowel sound and write **a** if the word begins with a consonant sound. Then write the word.

_____

_____

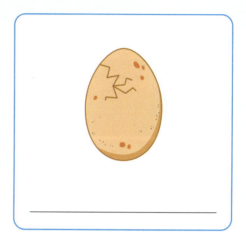

_____

_____

_____

_____

_____

_____

_____

Aa Ee Ii Oo Uu

ck

Action
Snap your fingers together in the air, and say *ck*.

red
win
drum
duck
neck
clock
lick
said
here
broomstick

Write a <ck> word in each chick and draw a picture to match.

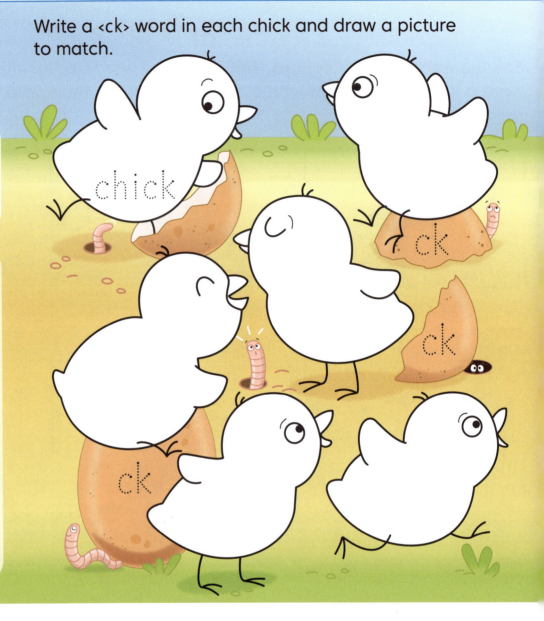

chick

ck

ck

ck

Dictation

1......................................

2......................................

3......................................

4......................................

5......................................

6......................................

7...

8...

9...

Plurals

Draw a picture for each word.

hats	pens	dog

cars	cow	frog

Write the word for each picture.

_____

_____

_____

_____

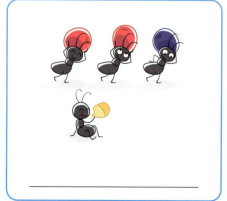

_____

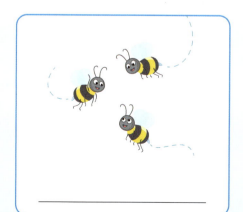

_____

Action
Fan yourself with your hand, and say *air*.

ox
run
from
air
hair
fair
chair
there
they
staircase

Write an <air> word in each hair piece and draw a picture to match.

hair

Dictation

1......................................

2......................................

3......................................

4......................................

5......................................

6......................................

7..

8..

9..

20

Plurals: ‹-s› and ‹-es›

Write the **plural noun** for each picture.
Then draw more of each picture to match.

birds _____

_____

_____

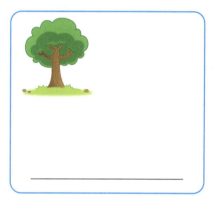

_____

_____

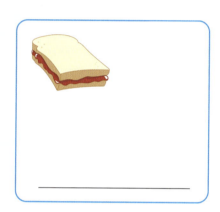

_____

Write the word for each picture.

_____

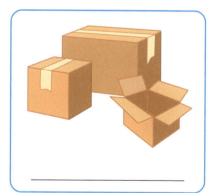

_____

_____

_____

_____

_____

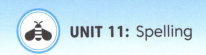

ear

Write an <ear> word in each pear and draw a picture to match.

Action
Fan yourself with your hand, and say *air*.

hop
fit
grin
bear
pear
tear
swear
go
no
wearing

Dictation

1.....................................

2.....................................

3.....................................

4.....................................

5.....................................

6.....................................

7...

8...

9...

22

Pronouns

Draw a picture for each pronoun. Remember to draw more than one person for the plural prounouns.

Singular pronouns

Singular pronouns

I
Point to yourself.

you
Point to someone else.

he
Point to a boy.

she
Point to a girl.

it
Point to the floor.

Plural pronouns

we
Point in a circle to include yourself and others.

you
Point to two other people.

they
Point to the class next door.

I

you

he

she

it

Plural pronouns

we

you

they

23

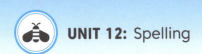

are

Action
Fan yourself with your hand, and say *air*.

bed
wet
prod
bare
care
rare
square
so
my
scarecrow

Write an ‹are› word in each scarecrow and draw a picture to match.

Dictation

1....................................

2....................................

3....................................

4....................................

5....................................

6....................................

7..

8..

9..

24

Initial consonant blends

Write the word underneath each picture.
All the words have initial consonant blends.

grin

_ _ _ _

_ _ _ _ _

_ _ _ _

_ _ _ _ _

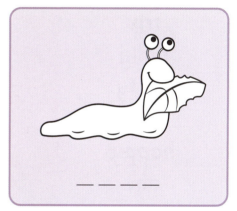

_ _ _ _

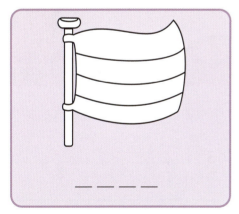

_ _ _ _

_ _ _ _

_ _ _ _

_ _ _ _ _

_ _ _ _ _

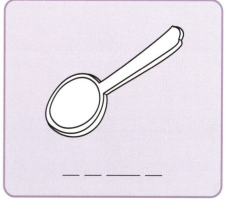

_ _ _ _ _

25

y

Action
Put your hands on your head, pointing them up like a donkey's ears, and say *ee*.

sad
let
trip
holly
party
story
happy
one
by
family

Write a word with <y> at the end in each holly leaf and draw a picture to match.

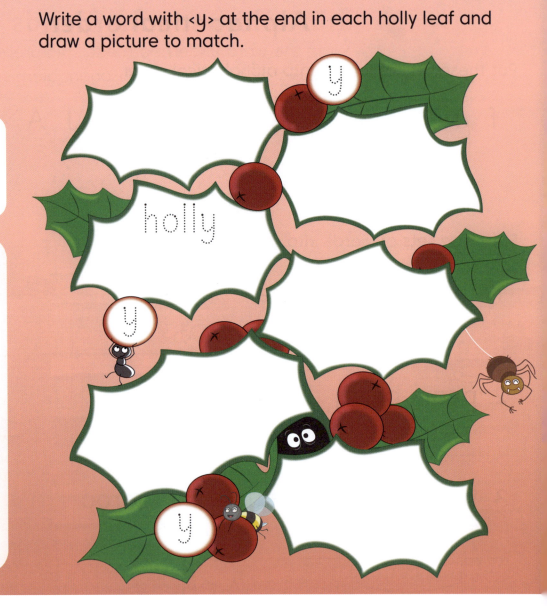

holly

Dictation

1....................................

2....................................

3....................................

4....................................

5....................................

6....................................

7..

8..

9..

26

Alphabetical order

Put these sets of letters into alphabetical order.

f d x o	u e n m	Q Z J A	C R Y G
_ _ _ _	_ _ _ _	_ _ _ _	_ _ _ _

Put these sets of words into alphabetical order.

1. Inky Snake Bee

   _____ _____ _____

2. pear berry lemon

   _____ _____ _____

3. hare wombat duck kangaroo

   _____ _____ _____ _____

4. van scooter truck helicopter

   _____ _____ _____ _____

ABCDEFGHIJKLMNOPQRSTUVWXYZ

Dictionaries tell you how a word is spelled and what it means. Use a dictionary to find the first word beginning with each of these letters.

D d _____   G g _____

N n _____   Z z _____

ran
hat
scar
cake
smile
nose
use
only
old
evening

Write a hop-over <e> word in each leaf and draw a picture to match.

sl_d_

pl_t_

tadp_l_

athl_t_

m_l_

Dictation

1 ....

2 ....

3 ....

4 ....

5 ....

6 ....

7 ....

8 ....

9 ....

Verbs

Action
Move your arms backward and forward at your sides, as if you are running.

Write the verb underneath each picture.

to _____

to _____

to _____

Draw a bee doing each verb.

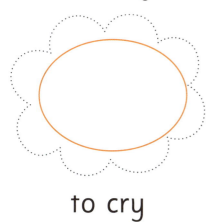

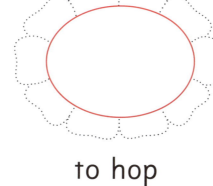

to cry

to hop

to brush

Think of three more verbs and draw them in the flowers.

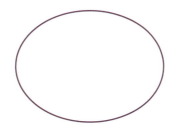

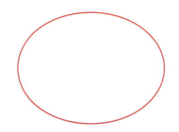

to _____

to _____

to _____

29

a_e
e_e
i_e
o_e
u_e

six
pad
smell
name
time
home
excuse
like
have
athlete

Write a hop-over <e> word in each leaf and draw a picture to match.

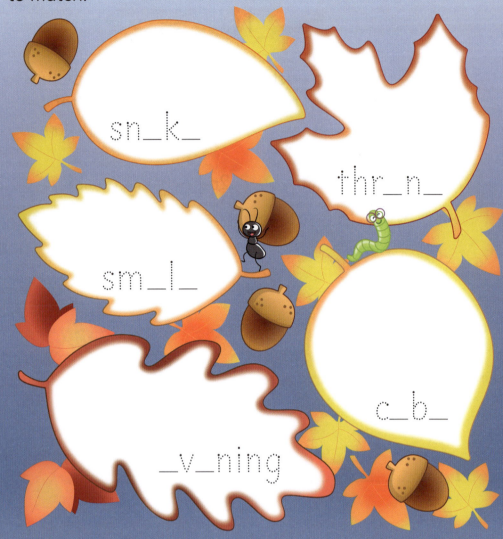

sn_k_

thr_n_

sm_l_

c_b_

_v_ning

Dictation

1.....................................

2.....................................

3.....................................

4.....................................

5.....................................

6.....................................

7...

8...

9...

30

Verbs

Think of a verb and write it on the line.

to _____

Write the verb next to each pronoun, and draw a picture to match. Remember that the verb has an <s> at the end when it is used after *he*, *she*, and *it*, and that you must draw more than one person for the plural pronouns.

1st person singular	2nd person singular	3rd person singular
		he / she / it
I _____	you _____	_____

1st person plural	2nd person plural	3rd person plural
we _____	**you** _____	**they** _____

31

ear

Action
Pull on your ears, saying *ear.*

cod
lot
snap
hear
dear
year
clear
live
give
earring

Write an ‹ear› word in each beard and draw a picture to match.

Dictation

1. ....

2. ....

3. ....

4. ....

5. ....

6. ....

7. ....

8. ....

9. ....

Verbs
past tense

Present tense action
Point toward the floor with the palm of your hand.

Past tense action
Point your thumb backward over your shoulder.

The simplest way to make the past tense is by adding <-ed> to the verb.

Today, I **talk**. talk + ed Yesterday, I **talked**.

If a verb already ends with an <e>, cross it out before adding <-ed>.

Today, I **smile**. smile + ed Yesterday, I **smiled**.

Put these verbs into the past tense.

Present	Past
jump	_____
paint	_____
like	_____
shout	_____
rest	_____

Present	Past
hope	_____
play	_____
wave	_____
skate	_____
twist	_____

Underline the verbs in red.
Then decide whether the sentences are in the present or the past.

She brushed her hair.	past / present
They look out of the window.	past / present
I cooked dinner.	past / present
The race started in the park.	past / present

33

ph

Action
Slowly bring your hands together, and say *ffffff*.

bus
pot
swim
phone
photo
graph
dolphin
little
down
alphabet

Write a <ph> word in each dolphin and draw a picture to match.

Dictation

1...................................

2...................................

3...................................

4...................................

5...................................

6...................................

7..

8..

9..

34

Verbs

hoped   hopped

Write these verbs in the simple past tense.

bat

_____

hop

_____

pat

_____

rip

_____

nod

_____

peg

_____

hug

_____

wag

_____

hum

_____

wh

Action
Blow onto your open hands, and say w.

did
cut
twin
whale
wheel
white
whisper
what
when
whenever

Write a <wh> word in each whale and draw a picture to match.

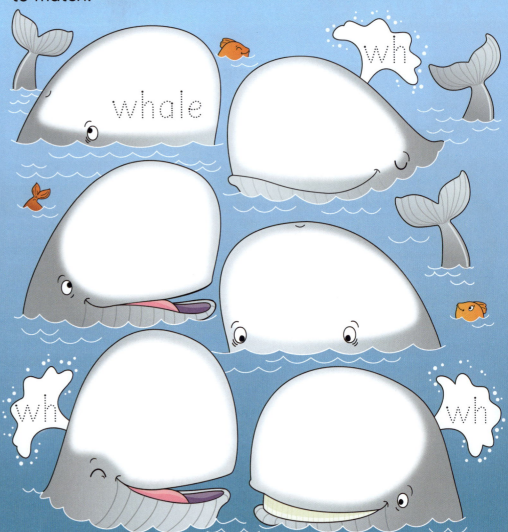

Dictation

1...

2...

3...

4...

5...

6...

7..

8..

9..

36

Verbs
the future

Action
Point to the front
with your finger.

Read the verbs in the *today* column. Then write the verbs in the past tense in the *yesterday* column, and in the future in the *tomorrow* column.

Past **yesterday**	Present **today**	Future **tomorrow**
I talked	I talk	I shall talk
I _____	I cook	I ____ _____
I _____	I listen	I ____ _____
I _____	I skate	I ____ _____
I _____	I walk	I ____ _____

Write some sentences about what you did yesterday.

_____

_____

_____

Write some sentences about what you will do tomorrow.

_____

_____

_____

ay

Write an ‹ay› word in each crayon and draw a picture to match.

crayon

Action
Cup your hand over your ear, and say *ai*.

an
cat
skin
say
away
play
today
why
where
playground

Dictation

1.....................................

2.....................................

3.....................................

4.....................................

5.....................................

6.....................................

7.....................................

8.....................................

9.....................................

38

Joining words and parts of sentences with *and*

Join the words and phrases together with **and**.

At the farm, we **jumped** and **played** in the hay.

We looked at the _____ ___ _____.

The cows were _____ ___ _____.

We picked _____ ___ _____.

We love **to have fun** ____ **help out at the farm!**

Think of two people you would like to see and two things you would like to do with them. Write them on the lines, and use **and** to join them.

Tomorrow, I will see _____ and _____.
We will _____ ___ _____.

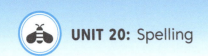

ea

Action
Put your hands on your head, pointing them up like a donkey's ears, and say *ee*.

met
web
spin
tea
heat
leaf
each
who
which
seashell

Write an ‹ea› word in each teapot and draw a picture to match.

Dictation

1....................................

2....................................

3....................................

4....................................

5....................................

6....................................

7..

8..

9..

40

Nouns

Write six nouns for the things you can see in the picture.

a _____   the _____

a _____   the _____

a _____   the _____

Underline the nouns in black. There can be more than one noun in a sentence.

1. The cow is black and white.

2. Jim drives a red and yellow tractor.

3. The sheep graze on the hills.

4. On Andrew's farm, there are cows, sheep, chickens, and a horse.

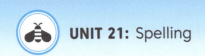

igh

Write an <igh> word in each light and draw a picture to match.

Action
Salute as if you are a sailor, and say *ie*.

lip
his
went
night
high
might
light
any
many
frightening

Dictation

1....................................

2....................................

3....................................

4....................................

5....................................

6....................................

7....................................

8....................................

9....................................

Adjectives

Action
Touch the side of your temple with your fist.

Color the snakes so that they match the adjectives.

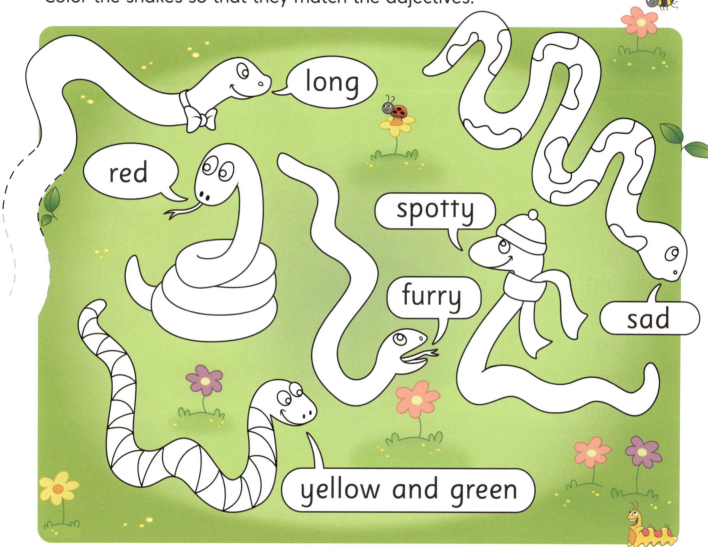

long

red

spotty

furry

sad

yellow and green

You can use more than one adjective at a time.
Color the snake to make it fit your description.

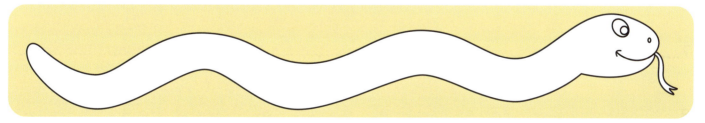

a _____, _____, _____ snake

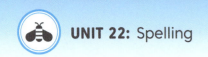

y

 **Action**
Salute as if you are a sailor, and say *ie*.

win
sit
stop
fry
dry
crying
sky
more
before
myself

Write a <y> word in each frying pan and draw a picture to match.

Dictation

1.....................................

2.....................................

3.....................................

4.....................................

5.....................................

6.....................................

7...

8...

9...

Comparatives and superlatives

Two of the most useful suffixes are <**-er**> and <**-est**>. They can be added to adjectives to make comparatives and superlatives.

Action
Touch the side of your temple with your fist.

Add the suffixes to the adjectives in Est-er Elephant and her friends. Remember to use the spelling rules.

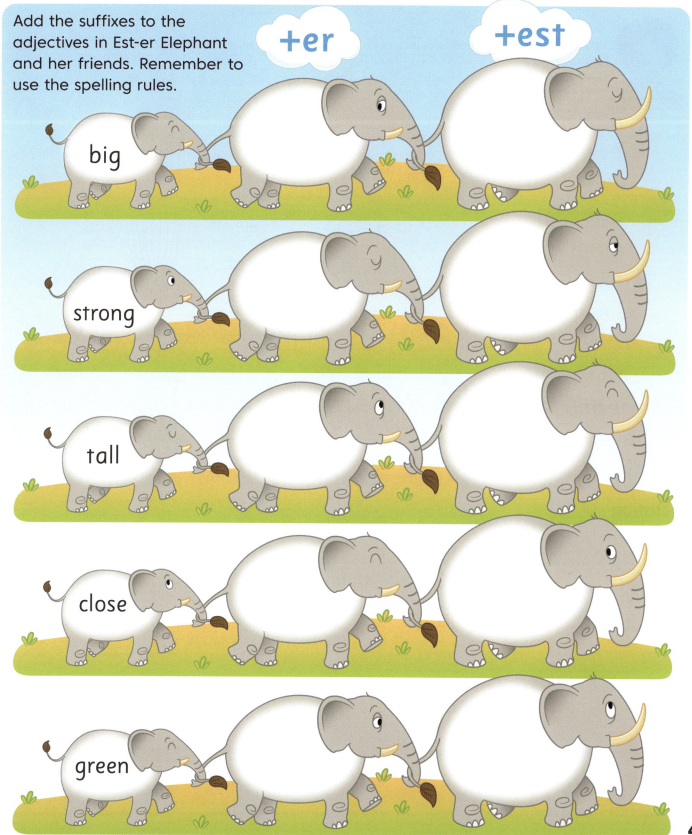

+er   +est

big

strong

tall

close

green

OW

Action
Bring your hand over your mouth, and say *oa*.

box
job
bulb
own
grow
elbow
yellow
other
were
snowman

Write an <ow> word in each snowman and draw a picture to match.

Dictation

1................................

2................................

3................................

4................................

5................................

6................................

7...

8...

9...

46

Final consonant blends

Read the final consonant blends and write inside them.
Use them to finish the words, and draw pictures to match.

mp	st	lt	nd	nt	sp

sta_____

po_____

be_____

a_____

ne_____

ha_____

la_____

cri_____

te_____

Write an <ew> word in each jewel and draw a picture to match.

Action
Point to people around you, and say *ue*.

Action
Move your head forward, and say *oo*.

bud

sun

held

few

flew

grew

chew

because

want

newspaper

Dictation

1......................................

2......................................

3......................................

4......................................

5......................................

6......................................

7...

8...

9...

Compound words

The compound word birds have muddled up their tails. Can you sort them out?
Color the tails to match the bodies.

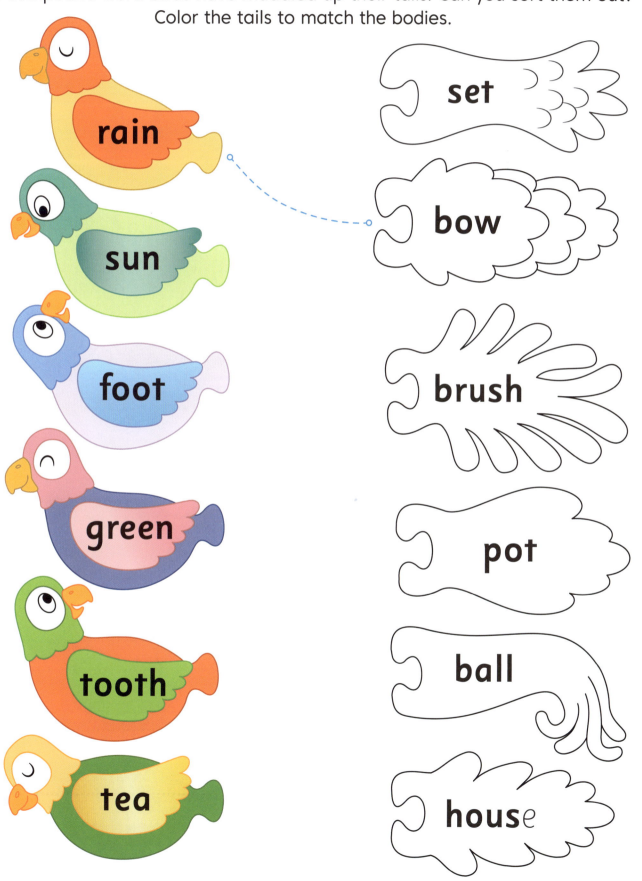

49

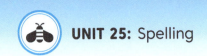

ou

Action
Pretend your finger is a needle and prick your thumb, saying *ou*.

bat

pet

self

out

our

round

mouth

saw

put

outside

Write an <ou> word in each house and draw a picture to match.

house

ou

ou

ou

Dictation

1...

2...

3...

4...

5...

6...

7...

8...

9...

Sequencing sentences

Write 1, 2, or 3 in the circles to show the order the sentences go in. Use the first set of pictures to help. Draw pictures in the other boxes to show what happens.

○ She could see big black clouds gathering in the sky.

○ Alex looked out of the window.

○ Soon rain began to fall, drumming against the window.

○ The seeds sprouted, grew tall, and made buds.

○ The buds opened into big yellow sunflowers.

○ The children had sowed some seeds.

1	2	3

○ Then they used a carrot for his nose.

○ Seth and Emma were making a snowman.

○ They made a body and a head with big balls of snow.

1	2	3

OW

Write an <ow> word in each owl and draw a picture to match.

Action
Pretend your finger is a needle and prick your thumb, saying *ou*.

big
fox
milk
how
owl
brown
town
could
should
flowerpot

Dictation

1.....................................

2.....................................

3.....................................

4.....................................

5.....................................

6.....................................

7...

8...

9...

52

Verbs

Write six verbs for the actions you can see in the picture.

to _____   to _____

to _____   to _____

to _____   to _____

Underline the verbs in red. There can be more than one verb in a sentence.

1. Jenny smiled at her friend.

2. Alex sails a boat.

3. Simran swims and dives in the sea.

4. The boys make a sandcastle and then play volleyball.

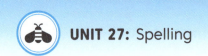

oi

Action
Cup your hands around your mouth, and say *oi*.

bug
had
film
oil
coin
noisy
toil
would
right
boiling

Write an <oi> word in each oil bottle and draw a picture to match.

Dictation

1......................................

2......................................

3......................................

4......................................

5......................................

6......................................

7..

8..

9..

54

Adverbs

Action
Bang one fist on top of the other.

Choose an adverb to go with each picture.

quickly   hungrily   slowly

softly   happily   loudly

Inky eats   Snake slithers   Bee buzzes

_____.   _____.   _____.

The ants whisper   The snail goes   The band played

_____.   _____.   _____.

55

oy

Write an <oy> word in each toy and draw a picture to match.

Action
Cup your hands around your mouth, and say *oi*.

jet
dig
help
boy
toy
enjoy
annoy
two
four
destroy

Dictation

1.....................................

2.....................................

3.....................................

4.....................................

5.....................................

6.....................................

7...

8...

9...

Suffixes

-s   -es   -ed   -er   -ing   -ly

peach ____   help ____   quick ____

paint ____   play ____   owl ____

Use all the suffixes to make new words and put each one into a sentence.

1. _____

2. _____

3. _____

4. _____

5. _____

6. _____

or

Write an <or> word in each horse and draw a picture to match.

Action
Put your hands on your head, pointing them down like a donkey's ears, and say *or*.

got
bun
belt
fork
storm
horse
forty
goes
does
morning

Dictation

1.....................................

2.....................................

3.....................................

4.....................................

5.....................................

6.....................................

7...

8...

9...

Making compound sentences with *and*

Which pairs of sentences go together? Make them into a compound sentence by joining them with *and*.

I met Jack at the park	_____ we visit him every year.
My uncle lives in Japan	_____ I ate pasta.
We went out for dinner	*and* we played on the slide.
Mabel likes horses	_____ she helps sick children.
My granny is a doctor	_____ her sister likes them too.

Make these pairs of simple sentences into compound sentences using *and*. Remember: when the simple sentences are joined together, they become clauses.

I run every morning. My dog comes with me.

_____

_____

Oscar fell over. His dad helped him up.

_____

_____

Can you write your own compound sentence using *and*?

_____

_____

al

Write an <al> word in each bubble and draw a picture to match.

Action
Pretend to turn a light switch on and off, and say o.

bad
vet
fact
all
talk
walk
small
made
their
beanstalk

Dictation

1......................................

2......................................

3......................................

4......................................

5......................................

6......................................

7...

8...

9...

Antonyms and the prefix ‹un-›

Write each opposite and draw a picture.

open _____

hot _____

up _____

white _____

day _____

asleep _____

Use the prefix ‹un-› to make the antonyms of these words.

un ____

do	<u>un</u>do	kind	_____
fair	___fair	pack	_____
friendly	___friendly	happy	_____

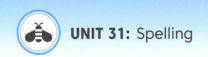

nk

Write an ‹nk› word in each drink and draw a picture to match.

When the sounds /ng/ and /k/ come together in a word, they are usually written as ‹nk›.

> fin
> sob
> left
> sink
> pink
> drink
> think
> once
> upon
> winking

drink

nk

nk

Dictation

1......................................

2......................................

3......................................

4......................................

5......................................

6......................................

7...

8...

9...

Using a dictionary

We can use a dictionary to check how to spell words.
Look up each word in your dictionary and circle the right spelling.

toofbrush
toothbrush

rabbit
rabit

starr
star

octopus
octapus

flouer
flower

buterfie
butterfly

These words are spelled incorrectly. Look them up and copy out the correct spelling.

boock   carpit   triangel

_____   _____   _____

We can use a dictionary to find out what a word means.
Look up these words and write down their meanings.

atlas _____

_____

yacht _____

_____

er

Action
Roll your hands over each other like a mixer, and say *er*.

mud
jam
sent
term
summer
river
number
always
also
woodpecker

Write an <er> word in each ginger cookie and draw a picture to match.

Dictation

1.....................................

2.....................................

3.....................................

4.....................................

5.....................................

6.....................................

7...

8...

9...

"Speech marks"

What noises are these animals making? Write the word for each noise in the speech bubble, and then write it again, inside the speech marks.

" _____ "

said the bee.

" _____ "

said the snake.

_____

said the bird.

_____

said the cow.

_____

said the donkey.

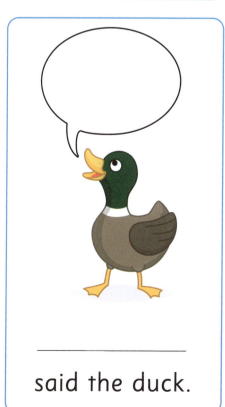

_____

said the duck.

ir

Action
Roll your hands over each other like a mixer, and say *er.*

yet
hid
wept
skirt
girl
shirt
first
of
eight
birthday

Write an <ir> word in each bird and draw a picture to match.

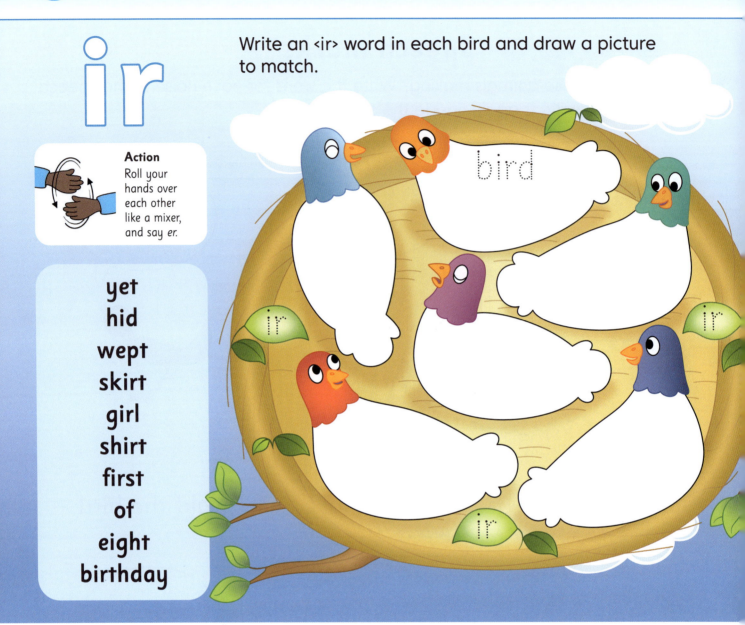

Dictation

1....................................

2....................................

3....................................

4....................................

5....................................

6....................................

7..

8..

9..

Word webs

How many words could you use instead of *said*? Write the words in the word web.

whispered

said

What words could be used instead of *sad*, or *cold*?

unhappy

sad

cool

cold

67

ur

Write a ‹ur› word in each turkey and draw a picture to match.

Action
Roll your hands over each other like a mixer, and say *er*.

not
sum
next
turn
nurse
turkey
purple
love
cover
hamburger

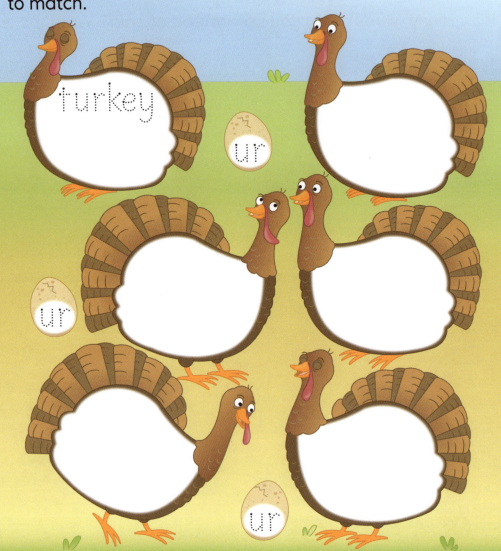

Dictation

1....................................

2....................................

3....................................

4....................................

5....................................

6....................................

7..

8..

9..

? ? ? ? ? **Questions** ? ? ? ? ?

We use these words to ask questions.

 ? what   why   when ?

where   who   which

Write inside the question marks, using different colors.

Answer these questions.

1. What is your name? _____

2. Where do you live? _____

3. When is your birthday? _____

If you met someone for the first time, what questions would you ask them?

_____

_____

_____

_____

_____

au

Write an <au> word in each astronaut and draw a picture to match.

Action
Pretend to turn a light switch on and off, and say *o*.

map
fix
jump
fault
pause
haunt
August
after
every
astronaut

Dictation

1..

2..

3..

4..

5..

6..

7...

8...

9...

70

? ? ? ? ? **Questions** ? ? ? ? ?

You ask questions to find things out.

what   where   when   why   who   which

Choose a question word to fit each sentence.

1. _____ won the quiz?

2. _____ time is it?

3. _____ book do you like best?

4. _____ are you going this summer?

5. _____ did you do that?

6. _____ can we play volleyball?

Read the questions and answers and see if you can guess which animal the girl is thinking of?

1. Do you have fur? Yes

2. How many legs do you have? Four

3. Do you have long ears? Yes

4. What do you eat? Carrots, oats, and hay

Which animal is it?

Find a partner and play the game yourself.

71

aw

Write an <aw> word in each saw and draw a picture to match.

Action
Pretend to turn a light switch on and off, and say *o*.

zip
men
pond
saw
claw
dawn
prawn
mother
father
strawberry

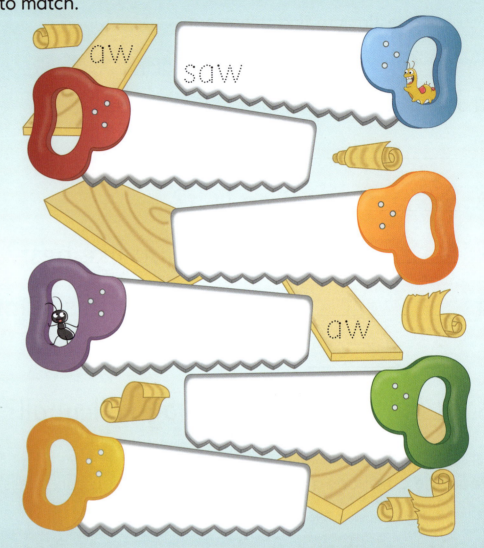

Dictation

1. ....

2. ....

3. ....

4. ....

5. ....

6. ....

7. ....

8. ....

9. ....

Parsing

Read the story below. Then underline the nouns in black and the verbs in red.

 Nouns

 Verbs

Inky toils long and hard in the garden. She digs the brown earth. The birds look at her closely. They wait eagerly for the grubs.

In the spring, Inky puts some seeds in the ground. She grows orange carrots, crispy lettuces, and tall, green beans. In summer, she carefully harvests the yummy vegetables and eats them.

Inky also grows tall, yellow sunflowers in the garden. She likes the lovely sunflowers. The birds also like the sunflowers. They hungrily eat the striped black and white seeds.

Now see if you can underline the pronouns in pink, the adjectives in blue, and the adverbs in orange.

 Pronouns
 Adjectives
 Adverbs

Spelling Tests

Spelling Test 1

1. _____
2. _____
3. _____
4. _____
5. _____
6. _____
7. _____
8. _____
9. _____
10. _____

Spelling Test 2

1. _____
2. _____
3. _____
4. _____
5. _____
6. _____
7. _____
8. _____
9. _____
10. _____

Spelling Test 3

1. _____
2. _____
3. _____
4. _____
5. _____
6. _____
7. _____
8. _____
9. _____
10. _____

Spelling Test 4

1. _____
2. _____
3. _____
4. _____
5. _____
6. _____
7. _____
8. _____
9. _____
10. _____

Spelling Test 5

1. _____
2. _____
3. _____
4. _____
5. _____
6. _____
7. _____
8. _____
9. _____
10. _____

Spelling Test 6

1. _____
2. _____
3. _____
4. _____
5. _____
6. _____
7. _____
8. _____
9. _____
10. _____

Spelling Test 7

1. _____
2. _____
3. _____
4. _____
5. _____
6. _____
7. _____
8. _____
9. _____
10. _____

Spelling Test 8

1. _____
2. _____
3. _____
4. _____
5. _____
6. _____
7. _____
8. _____
9. _____
10. _____

Spelling Test 9

1. _____
2. _____
3. _____
4. _____
5. _____
6. _____
7. _____
8. _____
9. _____
10. _____

Spelling Test 10

1. _____
2. _____
3. _____
4. _____
5. _____
6. _____
7. _____
8. _____
9. _____
10. _____

Spelling Test 11

1. _____
2. _____
3. _____
4. _____
5. _____
6. _____
7. _____
8. _____
9. _____
10. _____

Spelling Test 12

1. _____
2. _____
3. _____
4. _____
5. _____
6. _____
7. _____
8. _____
9. _____
10. _____

Spelling Test 13

1. _____
2. _____
3. _____
4. _____
5. _____
6. _____
7. _____
8. _____
9. _____
10. _____

Spelling Test 14

1. _____
2. _____
3. _____
4. _____
5. _____
6. _____
7. _____
8. _____
9. _____
10. _____

Spelling Test 15

1. _____
2. _____
3. _____
4. _____
5. _____
6. _____
7. _____
8. _____
9. _____
10. _____

Spelling Test 16

1. _____
2. _____
3. _____
4. _____
5. _____
6. _____
7. _____
8. _____
9. _____
10. _____

Spelling Test 17

1. _____
2. _____
3. _____
4. _____
5. _____
6. _____
7. _____
8. _____
9. _____
10. _____

Spelling Test 18

1. _____
2. _____
3. _____
4. _____
5. _____
6. _____
7. _____
8. _____
9. _____
10. _____

Spelling Test 19

1. _____
2. _____
3. _____
4. _____
5. _____
6. _____
7. _____
8. _____
9. _____
10. _____

Spelling Test 20

1. _____
2. _____
3. _____
4. _____
5. _____
6. _____
7. _____
8. _____
9. _____
10. _____

Spelling Test 21

1. _____
2. _____
3. _____
4. _____
5. _____
6. _____
7. _____
8. _____
9. _____
10. _____

Spelling Test 22

1. _____
2. _____
3. _____
4. _____
5. _____
6. _____
7. _____
8. _____
9. _____
10. _____

Spelling Test 23

1. _____
2. _____
3. _____
4. _____
5. _____
6. _____
7. _____
8. _____
9. _____
10. _____

Spelling Test 24

1. _____
2. _____
3. _____
4. _____
5. _____
6. _____
7. _____
8. _____
9. _____
10. _____

Spelling Test 25

1. _____
2. _____
3. _____
4. _____
5. _____
6. _____
7. _____
8. _____
9. _____
10. _____

Spelling Test 26

1. _____
2. _____
3. _____
4. _____
5. _____
6. _____
7. _____
8. _____
9. _____
10. _____

Spelling Test 27

1. _____
2. _____
3. _____
4. _____
5. _____
6. _____
7. _____
8. _____
9. _____
10. _____

Spelling Test 28

1. _____
2. _____
3. _____
4. _____
5. _____
6. _____
7. _____
8. _____
9. _____
10. _____

Spelling Test 29

1. _____
2. _____
3. _____
4. _____
5. _____
6. _____
7. _____
8. _____
9. _____
10. _____

Spelling Test 30

1. _____
2. _____
3. _____
4. _____
5. _____
6. _____
7. _____
8. _____
9. _____
10. _____

Spelling Test 31

1. _____
2. _____
3. _____
4. _____
5. _____
6. _____
7. _____
8. _____
9. _____
10. _____

Spelling Test 32

1. _____
2. _____
3. _____
4. _____
5. _____
6. _____
7. _____
8. _____
9. _____
10. _____

Spelling Test 33

1. _____
2. _____
3. _____
4. _____
5. _____
6. _____
7. _____
8. _____
9. _____
10. _____

Spelling Test 34

1. _____
2. _____
3. _____
4. _____
5. _____
6. _____
7. _____
8. _____
9. _____
10. _____

Spelling Test 35

1. _____
2. _____
3. _____
4. _____
5. _____
6. _____
7. _____
8. _____
9. _____
10. _____

Spelling Test 36

1. _____
2. _____
3. _____
4. _____
5. _____
6. _____
7. _____
8. _____
9. _____
10. _____

Aa Bb Cc Dd Ee

Ff Gg Hh Ii Jj Kk Ll Mm

Nn Oo Pp Qq Rr Ss

Tt Uu Vv Ww Xx Yy Zz